The
Ten Career
Commmandments

Practical books that inspire

Planning a Career Change
How to take stock, change course, and secure a better future for yourself

Handling Tough Job Interviews
Be prepared, perform well, get the job

Take Control of Your Own Career
Using NLP and other techniques to get the working life you want

High Powered CVs
Powerful application strategies to get you that senior level job

Please send for a free copy of the latest catalogue:

How To Books
3 Newtec Place, Magdalen Road,
Oxford OX4 1RE, United Kingdom
email: info@howtobooks.co.uk
http://www.howtobooks.co.uk

The
Ten Career
Commandments

Rob Yeung

howtobooks

Published in 2002 by
How To Books Ltd, 3 Newtec Place,
Magdalen Road, Oxford OX4 1RE, United Kingdom
Tel: (01865) 793806   Fax: (01865) 248780
e-mail: info@howtobooks.co.uk
www.howtobooks.co.uk

British Library Cataloguing in Publication Data.
A catalogue record for this book is available from
the British Library.

Produced for How To Books by Deer Park Productions
Typeset by PDQ Typesetting, Newcastle-under-Lyme, Staffordshire
Printed and bound in Great Britain by Bell & Bain Ltd, Glasgow

NOTE: The material contained in this book is set out in good faith for
general guidance and no liability can be accepted for loss or expense
incurred as a result of relying in particular circumstances on
statements made in the book. Laws and regulations are complex
and liable to change, and readers should check the current position
with the relevant authorities before making personal arrangements.

Contents

About the Author

Rob Yeung

Dr Rob Yeung is a consultant to international organisations on 'people issues'. He is a business psychologist at Kiddy and Partners, the leading firm of organisation consultants, where he works with individuals to develop their skills and careers. He was previously with The Boston Consulting Group, the international strategic management consultancy firm. He has written a number of books on management topics and he is frequently asked to contribute to the national press including *Financial Times* and *Daily Telegraph*, radio and television programmes such as CNN, as well as internet websites.

Preface

Have you ever wondered if there's more to working life than the daily grind of your job? Do you sometimes worry about where you're going and what you should be doing in five or ten years' time? Do you want to earn more money from your work? Do you ever wish you had a **career** and not just a job?

If you can answer yes to any one of these questions, then this book is for you. It's time to sit up and take action to get what you want.

Only a few decades ago, people could join one organisation and stay with it until they retired. They could wait for their parent-like company to send them on training courses, tell them what to do, hand them promotions on a plate and eventually usher them off to a happy retirement. An employee simply didn't have to make plans or take decisions to manage his or her career.

However, times have changed. Today's economic climate is much more competitive. What with cost-cutting drives, delayering, downsizing and even 'right-sizing', no one can be guaranteed a satisfying job for life. While most people will probably be able to find employment of some sort, it's not a given that it will be at all interesting or rewarding. So, it's up to you to do something about it.

But the good news is that you can determine the sort of career that you end up with. Organisations are desperate to recruit and retain the brightest and best employees. And if you're the sort of person who is willing to invest in acquiring the right skills and attitude, then companies will reward you with constantly challenging work – as well as hard cash – for your efforts.

If you're looking to take control of your career, then these ten career commandments are for you. Each chapter is filled with advice and exercises to make you think and change your working life for the better. Some of the exercises in each chapter may overlap with each other a bit so you don't necessarily have to do every single one. But if you can invest the time and effort to do them all properly, you'll find that you will get to know yourself so much better – which will mean that you'll be more likely to achieve your career goals.

This book is packed with ten big ideas to make a tremendous difference to your career. Good fortune!

Rob Yeung

1 Set Your Sights

*You need to know where you want
to go before you can get there.*

In this chapter:
- **Recognise your likes and dislikes**
- **Identify your priorities**
- **Understand your core values**
- **Write your eulogy**
- **Pull it all together**

No one can tell you what you should be doing with
your career. You can get advice and opinions from
friends, colleagues and family. But, at the end of the
day, you need to decide what your ideal job would be.

So here's four exercises to help you think about
what you could be enjoying and profiting from in the
future.

RECOGNISE YOUR LIKES AND DISLIKES

This first exercise is very simple. Just take a blank sheet
of paper and write down **all** of the tasks that you have

to do in an average month of your job. It might take you a while to think of every single activity you do but it's worth the effort to do it properly.

For example, a typical list could start as follows:

◆ Check e-mail.

◆ Open and read letters and deal with correspondence.

◆ Chair regular team meeting.

◆ Prepare presentation materials for meeting with customer.

◆ Make telephone calls to sales department.

◆ And so on.

Your list should be dozens and dozens of items long. Once you have your list, simply put a tick against the tasks you like doing. And (no prizes for guessing) put a cross against the tasks you don't like so much.

Now think about the following question:

> *What sorts of jobs would maximise your likes and minimise your dislikes?*

Okay, you're ready to move on to the next, more advanced exercise now.

IDENTIFY YOUR PRIORITIES

Look at the following list of 'motivators' and rank them in order of importance, starting with the things that are most important to you at the top. You could write each one on a Post-It note and then shuffle them around until you have a rank order that you are happy with. Or just take a blank sheet of paper and rewrite the list in order of your preferences.

- Colleagues
- Contribution to society
- Current income
- Family
- Friends
- Future earnings or equity ownership
- Geographical location
- Health
- Influence and power at work
- Leisure time
- Personal growth
- Predictable working hours
- Prestige and status
- Promotions
- Security
- Spiritual growth
- Spouse or partner
- Time to think and work alone
- Travel
- Working environment
- Your children

You're not allowed to have tied rankings – after all, life is sometimes about having trade-offs! If you want to make your millions, you'd better be prepared to give up your weekends. Or if you want to fulfil your personal ambition to travel the world, are you willing to slow your rise to the top? You can't, unfortunately, have your cake and eat it.

And check that the list really does represent what **you** want. Are you sure that you aren't just writing it thinking about what other people – your spouse, colleagues, or boss – would approve of?

Then write a brief description of how you would define each item. For example, someone's top three items might go as follows:

1. **Leisure time** – 'I am willing to work late in the evenings, but I never want to have to work on a weekend.'

2. **Equity ownership** – 'I want to have share options in any company that I work in.'

3. **Spouse** – 'I want to get married to Steve by the time I'm 35.'

When you've finished defining your list, look at it. What are the most important things in your life? And what isn't so important after all?

Let's think about it some more with the next exercise.

UNDERSTAND YOUR CORE VALUES

Do you ever think 'I wish I could be more like someone else?' Or perhaps that 'I'm glad I'm not like that person!'

Well, this next activity is designed to help you think quickly about your core values – the principles that you live to. Do you, for instance, think that we all need to be more socially responsible? Or perhaps you look up to people with an entrepreneurial nature?

Identify your heroes and villains

Write two columns on a sheet of paper. Write at the top of one column 'heroes and heroines'. The other column is for 'villains'.

Under the first column, write down a list of people that you admire – they could be living or dead, or even fictional. It could be famous business figures, film stars, political activists in the news or just people you've worked with.

Then, for each person, ask yourself:

◆ Why do you have such respect for these people? What attributes or traits do they have?

◆ In turn, what does that say about what you value?

And then do the opposite for the villains:

◆ What is it about these people that makes you scorn them?

◆ What implications does that have for your values?

WRITE YOUR EULOGY

How would you like to be remembered when you die? It may sound like an odd question, but it's a really useful way of helping you decide on your future goals and aspirations. And it somehow seems fitting at the beginning of your quest for a better career to be thinking about it from the very end!

Make sure that you have at least half an hour free from distraction – this exercise requires some serious thinking.

Here's your step-by-step guide to doing it:

◆ Take a clean sheet of paper and write at the top of the page 'My Eulogy: How I Would Like To Be Remembered'.

◆ Then write a detailed description of how you would like a close friend to describe you at your own funeral. Look back on the outputs of the previous two exercises for ideas.

◆ Think about your personal and family life. Think about your work. But don't forget about your social life and any artistic aspirations that you might have too.

◆ Don't limit yourself to what you have done so far. Think about the future too. Write about what you would **like** to achieve with the rest of your life.

Critique your eulogy

Once you've drafted your eulogy, take a break. Go do something else for a day or two. Then, discuss it with friends and family. Ask them what they think. Do you and they think that it suits your interests and talents?

Next, come back to make changes to it until you are satisfied with it. Most people find that it takes at least a couple of hours of serious thought – perhaps over the course of several weeks – to write a thorough eulogy.

The following is a list of groups of related adjectives that you can look at. The list is by no means comprehensive so feel free to add your own. On your second reading of your eulogy, which words might you want to add to it?

◆ Enterprising, autonomous, independent

◆ Artistic, creative, free

◆ Social, informing, knowledgeable

◆ Conventional, steady, realistic, disciplined, structured

◆ Persuasive, influential, trusted, leading, assertive

◆ Scientific, investigative, expert

When you've written your eulogy, read it through and think about the following questions:

◆ What are my goals in life?

◆ What are my goals in my work?

Write a newspaper article

If you don't like the idea of writing a eulogy, you could pretend that you are writing a magazine article celebrating your 75th birthday! Looking back on your life and career, what would the article say? And then think about these questions:

- What publication would you choose? And why?
- What sort of person are you aiming the article at?
- What key achievements does the article talk about?

PULL IT ALL TOGETHER

Finally, you're ready to think about and write a statement about your 'life mission'. It's worth doing because you'll have a sense of direction and will always know whether any career changes you make are compatible with what you want out of life.

> *Your life mission will act as a beacon on the sometimes dark road of your career journey.*

But your personal life mission isn't set in stone. You should revisit it whenever you make a big transition in your life – whether it's in your work or outside of it.

Here's a couple of example life missions:

◆ 'I want to build a career that focuses on challenge and excitement. And I think that I'll only ever be able to get that sense of challenge by working in small, entrepreneurial companies or start-up businesses. I'm willing to work very hard, but I want to be rewarded by promotions and financial benefits for it.'

◆ 'In my life, I want to balance my career against my family goals. I simply don't enjoy working long hours for the sake of it. I need to be able to enjoy the pleasures of life outside of my work. Whatever jobs I go for, I would always like to be able to take a full four weeks' holiday. Also, I want to be able to pick my children up from school at least twice a week and spend the whole evening with them.'

Now you're ready for the rest of this book, which deals with what your next career moves might be in order to achieve your goals.

REMEMBER TO...

✓ Think about what you do and don't enjoy about your job. Can you think of ways to improve your working life?

✓ Don't rush through these exercises. Take your time to think about them. And be honest about what you really want out of your life.

✓ Talk to friends, family, and colleagues about your goals. What advice can they give you about the direction your life might take?

2 Understand Your Talents

Skills, abilities, capabilities – what are yours?

In this chapter:
- **Recall your accomplishments**
- **Appraise yourself honestly**
- **Get a second opinion**

It's all very well having goals in mind. But do you have the skills you need to achieve your goals?

> *Knowing what you want will make you happy. But knowing what you're good at will make you successful.*

Chapter 1 helped you identify what you want out of your career. If you already have the skills you need to get there, that's great. But if you don't have the skills that you need, you can start to think about how you can go about acquiring them. So let's think about some different ways of getting an accurate picture of what you're good (or not so good) at.

RECALL YOUR ACCOMPLISHMENTS

Think back over your life and try to recall all of your major accomplishments. Again, it might help you to jot these down on a clean sheet of paper.

What have you achieved in your life that you're proud of? These can be in your work or outside of it. Don't forget areas such as:

◆ any sports you may participate in;

◆ hobbies and interests;

◆ academic achievements;

◆ community groups or charity work;

◆ clubs or societies you may belong to;

◆ personal triumphs.

> *Try to come up with at least one major accomplishment*
> *for every year of your life since you left school!*

Once you've done it, take a look at each item in turn, asking yourself:

- What was it about each one that made you feel pleased?

- What skills or talents did you use in completing each of your accomplishments?

Write a log of your life

As a double check to make sure that you haven't forgotten any of your significant achievements, you might want to write a retrospective log of your life.

It's a very simple exercise. Begin by taking a notebook or several dozen fresh sheets of paper. Write the current year at the top of the first page, then last year's date on the next page, and the previous year's date on the page after that. Carry on until you have got to the year that you left school.

Now, for each year, write down the answers to the following questions:

- Where were you working? Or what were you doing that year?

- Where were you living?

- Who were the major influences on your life that year?

Once you've answered these questions, use your notes to remind you about the significant accomplishments or achievements that you made in that year. Compare it to the previous list you made – did you miss anything out the first time round?

An alternative exercise is to take a large sheet of paper and draw a graph of your life since you left school. The *X*-axis (the horizontal line, going from left to right) represents the years of your life. And the *Y*-axis (the vertical dimension) is a measure of how good or bad the year was – the higher up the page the line goes, the better it was.

You might end up with a graph like so:

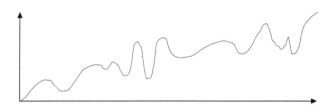

Now, think about the following questions:

◆ For each of the 'peaks' in the graph – your high points – why was it a high? What skills did you use that made it a high? How did the events of the time relate to your values?

◆ For your low points – the troughs in the graph – what happened? Why was it a low? What did you learn about yourself and your values? Were there any lessons about what you should avoid in the future?

APPRAISE YOURSELF HONESTLY

It's important to understand what you're good at – but it's twice as important to understand your areas of weakness too. Once you understand what you're not so good at, you can either work to develop and strengthen those areas, or make sure that you take your career in a direction that allows you to avoid your areas of weakness.

The following list of questions is based on research done at Harvard Business School. Go through each of the questions and score yourself from one to ten (1 = very poor, 5 to 6 = average, 10 = exceptional) for each skill or 'competency'. Then try to think about examples of why you are good or bad at each one to use as 'evidence' for your score.

> *Be really honest with yourself.*
> *No one can be good at everything!*

- **Achievement-orientation** – to what extent are you someone who strives to gain personal, professional, and academic achievements?

- **Interpersonal skills** – how good are you at communicating, getting on with other people and working in teams?

- **Influence and persuasion** – how good are you at negotiating, cajoling, asserting yourself and getting what you want from other people?

- **Flexibility** – how good are you at adapting to new situations and sudden changes of circumstance?

- **Expertise/technical proficiencies** – what are your areas of specialist knowledge?

- **Reasoning** – how good are you at solving problems and making difficult decisions?

- **Business awareness** – to what extent do you understand the commercial or market issues that affect your work?

- ◆ **Control** – how good are you at leading other people, delegating work and exerting your authority when necessary?

Now look at your ratings and the examples you have collected as evidence for your scores. Firstly, do you think the scores are a **fair** and **honest** appraisal of your own skills? Now compare your list of skills to your life mission statement from Chapter 1 – do you have the skills you need to achieve your career goals? And, if not, how will you **get** those skills?

GET A SECOND OPINION

It's possible to have a blind spot about your own strengths and weaknesses. Personal insecurity may prevent you from recognising some of your strengths – but sometimes a bit of over-confidence can mask your own weaknesses too.

One of the most valuable activities you can do is to get some input from people who know you well. Choose a half-dozen people – or 'respondents' – to give you some feedback.

Choose respondents carefully

Don't just pick people who unconditionally love you – sometimes family and friends aren't the right people to tell you about your weaknesses. You need to choose people who:

◆ you think will be honest with you;

◆ you have respect for and listen to.

So try to pick a variety of people from different spheres of your life:

◆ current colleagues;

◆ ex-colleagues;

◆ an ex-boss or maybe your current manager (if you have a good relationship);

◆ a couple of friends and family members.

Respondents can be wary of appearing to be over-critical of you. So you need to give them licence to talk about not only your strengths but also your weaknesses. You might want to think carefully about a 'script' for what you might say to each person.

You might want to:

◆ Explain that you are trying to make some career plans, and explain that you would really appreciate their honest opinion.

◆ Ask: 'What do you think my strengths are?'

◆ Ask: 'What do you think my areas of weakness are? What could I do better?'

◆ Whether you agree with the feedback you get or not, make sure that you don't react negatively – angrily or sulkily – to their feedback.

◆ Thank them for their time and effort.

> *How do other people's perceptions of your strengths and weaknesses compare with your own appraisal?*

Ring round

As a quick (but not so insightful) alternative to talking to these various people in person, just consult your address book. Pick up the telephone and ring twenty people that know you well. Get a sample of different people – friends and family, colleagues and business acquaintances. And then ask them:

◆ 'What do you think is my greatest skill or ability?'

Write down the responses and look at whether there are any patterns. It's as simple as that.

REMEMBER TO

✓ Take your time to think about all your skills. Which of your skills do you **enjoy** using?

✓ Be **honest** with yourself in considering your weaknesses – there's no point pulling the wool over your own eyes when it comes to your career.

✓ Get some advice from people who know you well. But bear in mind that family and friends may not be as candid as you really need them to be.

3 Make It Happen

Don't just wish and dream – get out there and do it.

In this chapter:
- **Take one step at a time**
- **Identify your constraints**
- **See yourself as others see you**
- **Go for the grand plan**
- **Celebrate success**

Now let's think about how you might be able to achieve your career goals. It's time to plan the steps that you will take to get what you want.

Don't worry if your career goals at first seem a bit too daunting to achieve. If you can break your career goals up into a number of steps to take, it will seem a lot more straightforward.

But I'm not going to say that it will be easy. It may take years of building up your skills and changing jobs a few times to get the kind of career that you want.

TAKE ONE STEP AT A TIME

Don't just sit there reading this book – take action! If you've read through Chapters 1 and 2, you should already have a bucketful of ideas about what sort of career you want and the sorts of skills you have (or don't have).

What are the things that you can change immediately – from tomorrow, in fact?

Don't keep putting if off. Do something today.

Take just a few minutes now to think about the things that you could stop, start, and continue doing. Don't worry if you aren't sure how you can achieve them – it's more important just to start getting your ideas down on paper:

I will STOP (i.e. things that I don't like about myself):

◆

◆

I will START (i.e. things that I would like to improve):

◆

◆

I will CONTINUE (i.e. good things about myself that I must persist with):

◆

◆

Copy the list out and put it somewhere prominent – on your fridge or next to your computer or bathroom mirror, perhaps. And see how you're doing in two weeks' time.

IDENTIFY YOUR CONSTRAINTS

We all have barriers and obstacles that stand in the way of achieving our career goals. Once you have identified these, you can try to figure out how to overcome them. So let's think about yours.

Constraints fall into a number of broad areas. Think about the following areas in turn and try to analyse your personal situation.

- **Skills**. Do you have the skills you need?

- **Experience**. Do you have the right work experience? Do you have the right number of years of experience on your CV? Are there qualifications that you might need?

- **Family**. What are the needs of your spouse or 'significant other'? What do your family and any children need from you?

- **Finances**. Do you need to pay for further education or training to achieve your goals? How will you afford it?

- **Location**. Are you tied to a particular geographical location?

- **Physical health**. Are you in good health? Do you have the energy to pursue your goals? Or do you have any illnesses or physical conditions that you need to factor into the equation?

> *What other constraints are getting in the way of you achieving your career aspirations?*

Now look at your constraints.

◆ Which ones can you do something about? And what can you do about tackling them in order to achieve your career goals?

◆ Which constraints can you not change? If you honestly think that you can't change them, do you perhaps need to change your career goals at all?

SEE YOURSELF AS OTHERS SEE YOU

One particular constraint that can hold you back is the way that other people see you. For instance, you may see yourself as an ambitious and confident person – but others may see you as ruthless and arrogant! Or you may think of yourself as honest and caring – again, others could view you as tactless and smothering.

> *People's perceptions are rarely the same as your own perceptions of yourself.*

There are many reasons other people may have these rather odd perceptions about us. They could, for instance, simply misunderstand the reasons you behave the way you do. Or maybe they just made up their minds about you long ago based on a first impression that isn't the real you.

Whatever the reasons though, perceptions are a double-edged sword. So it's important for you to understand how other people's perceptions might hold you back from getting what you want.

Look at the following list of adjectives. Choose the ones in the left-hand column that you think describe you. Then read the adjective in the right-hand column and try to think whether there might be any circumstances in which other people might think of you in that less positive light.

- ◆ Ambitious = Ruthless
- ◆ Confident = Arrogant
- ◆ Assertive = Bullying
- ◆ Extraverted = Loud
- ◆ Tough = Uncaring
- ◆ Independent = Isolated

If none of those adjectives seem to describe you, have a look at the next set:

◆ Practical   =   Unimaginative

◆ Cautious   =   Indecisive

◆ Spontaneous =   Disorganised

◆ Thorough   =   Obsessive

◆ Tolerant   =   Uncaring

◆ Realistic   =   Pessimistic

Or maybe try the last list:

◆ Honest   =   Tactless

◆ Fun   =   Frivolous

◆ Caring   =   Meddlesome

◆ Trusting   =   Gullible

◆ Supportive =   Submissive

◆ Honourable =   Moralistic

◆ Loyal   =   Servile

What adjectives would you use to describe yourself? Try to think for yourself about the flip-side of how others might perceive you.

In trying to achieve your career goals, make sure you don't fall into the trap of having others misinterpret your actions or misjudge you.

GO FOR THE GRAND PLAN

Breaking down your overall career goal into a series of smaller, more achievable sub-goals will help you to get there. It's like planning a journey from where you live to somewhere you've never driven before. Simply knowing that you need to 'drive to Glasgow' doesn't actually help you to get there. But breaking it down – 'drive to the local town centre, then locate the main road, drive ten kilometres, then get onto the motorway until you get to Junction 10...' and so on – will clarify the steps you need to take, making it easier to achieve your overall goal.

Devise your action plan

Try to break your career goals into the sub-goals that you need to take. And for each sub-goal, think about the following questions:

- ◆ **What** do you plan to achieve?

- ◆ **How** will you go about achieving it? What will you actually do?

- ◆ **Who** else might you need to get involved? What support or intervention can they offer you?

- ◆ **When** will you do this? Is it something that you can do quickly – or is it something much longer-term?

Once you've done this, you will have a draft action plan. You will never have a finalised and definitive action plan because, as the weeks and months pass, you will need to keep checking that your actions are still appropriate.

For instance, you may be doing something completely different in a year's time from what you do now. If that's the case, you will need to go back to Chapter 1 to rethink your life mission, and then come back to this chapter to think about the implications for your action plan.

And, as you read the further chapters of this book, hopefully you will get more and more ideas about the kinds of skills you need and the activities you should engage in to help you achieve your career goals. So you will need to revisit this section several times to keep updating your plan of action.

CELEBRATE SUCCESS

One of the most important parts of your plan is the answer to the question: 'When will you do this?'

If you've set yourself reasonable dates to complete each of the sub-goals in your action plan, you can monitor your progress.

If you miss your own deadline dates, you need to ask yourself:

◆ Why did I miss the deadline?

◆ What can I do to catch up with my plan?

◆ Are there other parts of my plan that this affects?

On the other hand, when you do achieve a sub-goal on time:

◆ Go back to your action plan and put a big tick next to the sub-goal. Well done – you have completed part of your career journey.

◆ And then go out and celebrate. Get your partner to take you out for dinner or spend some money on something that you deserve!

REMEMBER TO

✓ Avoid putting it off – even if you can only come up with a few, small actions to improve your working life. But ideally, you should devise an action plan to help you achieve your career goals.

✓ Consider the barriers and obstacles in your life that prevent you from achieving your goals. How can you overcome them?

✓ And keep coming back to your action plan. Plans are only useful if they are kept up to date.

4 Get Your Own Way

*Convincing, cajoling and commanding
others are probably the most critical skills
you will ever need in your career.*

In this chapter:
- ◆ **Make the right impact**
- ◆ **Influence others**
- ◆ **Negotiate for what you want**

Quite often, your career goals are dependent on other people. Perhaps it's your boss who can make the decision whether to send you on a course or give you the project you want. Or maybe it's your bank manager deciding whether or not to lend you the money to start up your own business.

So when it's people who make the key difference between helping you or holding you back, how can you influence and persuade them to give you what you want?

MAKE THE RIGHT IMPACT

Psychological research tells us that most people will make up their minds on whether to help or hinder you based on whether they **like** you or not. It's not a very sophisticated way of making a decision – it's just human nature. So you need to make a good impression on others to ensure that they like you.

People give opportunities to the people they like best

In addition, most people actually make up their minds about other people in the first three to five minutes of meeting someone. And then they tend to be very reluctant to change their opinions once they have pigeon-holed you in their mind. So it doesn't give you much margin for error.

In my work as a business psychologist, I interview a lot of people for jobs. And it never ceases to **amaze** me how poorly some people can come across initially – and the worst thing is that they don't seem to realise it either! Below are some tips for making those critical first minutes count.

Create a great first impression

Sort out your physical **appearance**. Get the opinion of someone you trust and ask them about your dress sense. Too young and trendy – even too colourful or too tarty? Or are you dressing old before your time? And get a good haircut while you're at it.

Develop a confident **handshake and smile**. Other people really do notice a limp or vice-like handshake. Similarly, they notice shyness and a failure to make eye contact as much as they hate over-boisterousness or insincerity.

Practise **asking** good questions and **listening** to the answers. Always have a couple of questions up your sleeve to ask other people. Other people will always think that you are a good conversationalist if you let them do all the talking!

Now ask the people you know: what tips do they have for making a great first impression?

INFLUENCE OTHERS

Exercising influence over others is a subtle skill. Usually, you're trying to persuade someone as to the merits of something when there may be no right or wrong answer.

There are three broad styles of influence. Most people tend to use one much more than any other. There is no style that is 'best' at all times. Quite simply, if one doesn't work, you should try another.

Read the three types below and ask yourself:

◆ Which style do you use most often?

◆ When you are next trying to influence someone, would adopting a different style help you get what you want?

Convince others

Is this you?

◆ I enjoy using facts and figures to back up my arguments.

◆ Typically, I find it easy to criticise the suggestions of other people.

◆ I usually focus on pros and cons, costs and benefits.

Convincers tend to focus on logic and reason. They think through the merits and disadvantages of an argument. And it's a particularly good style when you are trying to present an argument with tangible goals and outcomes.

Cajole others

Is this you?

◆ I try to listen to people's concerns before putting forward my ideas.

◆ I show my appreciation for other people by praising their good achievements.

◆ I try to put myself into other people's shoes to find out what makes them tick.

Cajolers focus on making others feel valued. They focus on the needs of other individuals rather than the needs of the task at hand itself.

Cajoling can be a good style of persuasion when the logic behind your argument isn't cut and dried enough or convincing to work.

Command others

Is this you?

- I sometimes tell people to do things and then explain it to them later on.

- At times, I rely on my position or authority to get things done.

- I tend to point out the mistakes in what other people are doing.

Commanders tend to tell people what to do. They set goals for others and expect them to complete their assigned tasks.

This style is especially appropriate when there's an emergency or when time is short. After all, a fireman trying to evacuate a burning building shouldn't have to waste time convincing or cajoling people to leave the building!

In fact, there is nothing 'good' or 'bad' about any of the three styles. Try to modify your style to adapt to different people and different situations.

NEGOTIATE FOR WHAT YOU WANT

Even the most persuasive person in the world can sometimes fail to get what they want. You may have presented your case in a logical manner, listened to their doubts – and the other person can still refuse to agree with you. Now it's time to negotiate.

Negotiation is simply what you do when you need to **make trade-offs** to come to an agreement with someone else who initially does not agree with you. To begin with, the other person may not be willing to give you what you want – or you may not be willing to give them what they want.

It's a key skill for helping you achieve your career goals – for example when you're changing jobs and negotiating a salary and benefits package, or when you are bargaining over the price of a product or service. And here's how to do it in five steps.

1. Determine your objectives

Negotiation is often pictured as psychological warfare – two sides sticking rigidly to their positions, trying to avoid conceding for fear of 'losing face', and bitterly wearing the other side down in the hopes of 'winning'.

But it will be far more useful for you if you can look at it as a process whereby you trade off some of your more superficial **wants** to ensure that you get what you **need**.

So, prepare by working out in your own mind:

◆ What do you **want**? What, in an ideal world, would you like to get out of the discussion?

◆ What do you **need**? What is the minimum that you are willing to accept?

◆ Why should the other party give you what you want? What are the **reasons** or justifications to back up your demands?

◆ What minor **concessions** are you willing to make to ensure you both get an agreement?

Let's take a salary negotiation as an example. You've decided that you would like to work for Company X and they have offered you a salary of £36,000. In an ideal world, you'd like a salary of £42,000. But you realise that you want very much to work for this company – so would actually be willing to put up with a salary of only £38,000 because the job would be such good experience for your long-term career.

2. Identify the other person's position

When you meet the other party, you need to explain your position – based on your wants and the reasons behind those wants.

Then you need to ask some questions to find out what they are willing to offer you in return.

3. Look for common ground

In order to show that the negotiation isn't a battle and that you're not just arguing for the sake of being difficult, it's worth taking a few minutes to emphasise what you already agree on.

For example, in the salary negotiation, you might say something like: 'We've established that I'd like to work here and that you would like me to work here too.'

4. Agree compromises

Now that you've established each other's initial wants, you can probe a bit further to find out **why** they have made the offer they are making. You could, for example, ask: 'Can I ask you why you won't go higher/lower?'

And once they explain their reasons, you can suggest some conditions to getting an agreement, using questions such as:

◆ 'I understand that, but I can't do X – but what if I do Y instead?'

◆ 'What if I were to do X – would you do Y in return?'

◆ 'I'm willing to concede X, but would you do Y for me instead then?'

5. Close the deal

There's nothing worse than leaving a negotiation only to receive a written offer that doesn't match up to what you thought you'd bargained for! So check that you both agree by summarising what has happened.

Finally, this is the stage when the paperwork and legal stuff gets handled. If it's a job that you're negotiating around, you should expect a written contract. Or if it's around payment for a product or service, perhaps a purchase order or invoice will be necessary.

REMEMBER TO

✓ Prepare as much as you can before meeting people – you only have about three minutes to impress them, so don't screw it up.

✓ Keep in mind the different styles of persuading people to give you what you want – remember that no one style is right all of the time.

✓ But don't waste energy arguing with people who won't give you what you want. Invest some thought in how you will *negotiate* with them instead.

5 Boost Your Skills

Continuing Professional Development is today's big buzz-phrase. Are you doing enough of it?

In this chapter:
- **Work *across* teams**
- **Get qualified**
- **Learn new skills**
- **Broaden your horizons**

If your career involves having to work in organisations with other people, then there are some general skills that will really help you to climb that career ladder. It doesn't matter if you work with just 20 people or 20,000 people – the skills are still the same.

And even if your career goal is to work for yourself eventually, some of the following skills are still worth pursuing, as they will help you to impress future customers or clients.

WORK *ACROSS* TEAMS

Teamworking is yesterday's news. Who doesn't already know that it's important to get on with the people you work with?

Nowadays, it's a given that you'll be able to work with the people in your own team. What employers want next is the ability to work with other teams.

Increasingly, business involves working across departments, divisions and even countries. If you have been in your current role for more than two or three years, you really should try at least one of the following:

◆ Get a transfer to another department, ideally. Even if you can't progress up the ladder, it's better to move laterally to develop your skills.

◆ Try asking for a temporary secondment to another department if you can't get a permanent transfer.

◆ Or at least get involved in a project that involves extensive liaison with people outside of your own department.

Now have a think: who should you approach to get some experience of working across teams?

Work in virtual teams

Relatedly, teams can actually be spread over huge geographical distances. In the age of the mobile phone, fax, and email – a lot of teams don't actually spend very much time face-to-face with each other.

The challenge for today's employee is to get to grips with all of the important communication technology. But just because the technology is there doesn't mean that it should be abused.

Some tips for being a savvy virtual teamworker:

◆ Think about how often you use e-mail versus voicemail versus telephone versus face-to-face contact for communication. Don't rely on any one of these too much.

◆ If you need to criticise someone, **always** do it face to face. Using technology is just plain cowardly.

◆ Use the telephone or a personal visit when you need something done urgently. E-mail is better when it's less urgent and you don't want to bother people right then and there.

What other rules of technology etiquette exist where you work?

GET QUALIFIED

When was the last time you picked up a professional qualification? It shows future employers that you are committed to developing yourself. And if you want to work for yourself, it will show your future customers or clients that you are competent and credible in your chosen field.

Which of the following options might apply to you?

◆ Chartered or certified status.

◆ Diplomas.

◆ Master's degrees or an MBA.

◆ Distance learning (e.g. Open University) courses.

◆ Membership of a relevant professional body, association or society.

If you do decide to embark on a course of further study, consider whether you would be better suited to doing it full-time or part-time. Are you someone who can cope with studying in the evenings after a full day of work? On the other hand, if you decide to study full-time, how would you support yourself financially?

> *As a rule of thumb, try to pick up a professional qualification at least every five years.*

LEARN NEW SKILLS

But employers don't just look for professional development – they also like to see personal development. Learning skills outside work will make you more employable – it shows future employers that you'll pick up quickly on whatever training they might want to put you through.

There are hundreds of skills you could learn. Have you ever considered taking up:

♦ a musical instrument?

♦ a sport or physical activity – from aerobics to abseiling?

♦ a foreign language?

♦ an expertise that challenges gender roles – such as car maintenance if you're a woman or cookery if you're a man?

♦ leading a team – such as voluntary work for charity or committee responsibilities for a club or society?

> *New skills liven up CVs.*

BROADEN YOUR HORIZONS

Employers sometimes complain that employees don't have enough understanding of what is happening outside their particular career specialism. For example, marketing people don't tend to know enough about HR issues, and sales people frequently don't appreciate the pressures that finance departments can face.

> *Do you read a 'quality' newspaper at least three or four times a week?*

Consequently, read outside your area of expertise – even if it's just skimming through the *Financial Times* once a week at your local library. It'll broaden your knowledge and give you at least a passing familiarity with the world of business – a very useful skill when you're being interviewed for a new job and when the interviewer could potentially engage you in business chit-chat.

Use the World Wide Web

There is a lot of useful information out there. But buying lots of books can be expensive as information on work and careers gets outdated very quickly. So try to get yourself access to the internet.

Do some searching for articles and information to advance your career. Two particularly good search engines for getting career-related material are:

◆ **www.northernlight.com** – which features a large index and collects documents from newswires, magazines and a variety of databases;

◆ **www.google.com** – considered by many people to be the best search engine on the World Wide Web.

Or some useful websites you might want to look at include:

◆ **www.indsoc.co.uk** – the website of the Industrial Society, a not-for-profit organisation offering advice on topics as wide ranging as employment law to skills development;

- **www.learndirect.co.uk** – a site aimed at promoting life-long learning among both businesses and individuals by providing a range of learning opportunities;

- **www.globeroom.com** – offers information and free subscription to a magazine on how to get more out of working life;

- **www.flametree.com** – targets people interested in work/life balance;

- **www.trainingzone.co.uk** – has a list of workshops and courses that you can complete on-line.

REMEMBER TO

✓ Keep exposing yourself to new challenges at work. The more you are challenged at work, the more quickly you will learn and eventually achieve your career goals.

✓ Don't just think about development as being limited to work. Personal growth is important too.

✓ Read voraciously! Pick up newspapers and surf the internet to gather as much information about the world of work as possible.

6 Thrive On Change

Change or die.

In this chapter:
- **Embrace personal change**
- **Get involved in change**
- **Help others in uncertain times**

We can't stop change from intervening in our lives. Psychologists have found that transitions in our lives can trigger a pattern of reactions and feelings. Thankfully, we also understand how to minimise the often disruptive effects of change.

But employers are also desperate to find people who can make change happen. In today's increasingly competitive world, companies are always looking for people who can act as agents of change.

> *Accepting change and helping others through it will really help your career to fly.*

EMBRACE PERSONAL CHANGE

Change comes in many forms in our lives. These transitions can vary from moving into a new house or winning the lottery to an untimely death in the family or a divorce. On the career front, significant changes include promotions to accepting a new job. But even the introduction of a new person to a close-knit team can be disruptive.

So how can you get to grips with change more readily?

Deal with negative feelings

Some tried and tested methods for reducing the stress of change are:

◆ **Remember change is double-edged**. Change is rarely only good or only bad. Take, for example, a woman who gets promoted – she might be excited at first, but soon realise that she's out of her depth and then find herself working long hours to cope with the pressures of the new role. Or a man who is made redundant – initially he might be depressed but eventually realise it's an opportunity to embark on a new career path.

◆ **Keep things in perspective**. Even when a change seems positive – a pay rise or a promotion, for example – it's natural to wonder whether you're up to it and to feel stressed by it. The important thing is to remember that you will get through it. In a year's time, you'll probably be looking back on the event and be able to laugh at it. No matter how tough things might be at the start of a change event, it **will** get better.

◆ **Distract yourself if you're feeling down**. In those dark moments of despair, the worst thing you can do is spend time on your own thinking too much. Do some physical exercise, listen to some uplifting music, make a phone call – anything to take your mind off things for a while.

Draw on other people

The people around you can act as a buffer against the stress of change too. You can use them to help if you:

◆ **Disclose to others**. Disclosing is just another way of saying that you should talk to other people. Don't bottle it up and feel that you have to cope with change alone. Talk to your colleagues, friends and family. And be honest with your feelings.

◆ **Act on advice**. Amazingly, people going through a transition in their lives often try to struggle through using only their own brain. The people around you will have good ideas for how you can get through a period of change. If it's a good change, the people around you can ground you and make sure you don't get carried away. If it's a change for the worse, they can give you pointers on how to get through it more quickly.

GET INVOLVED IN CHANGE

In an increasingly competitive world, organisations both big and small are obsessed with 'change management' – revamping systems, processes, and ways of working to meet the needs of increasingly demanding customers.

Devoting some time to getting involved in a change project has two main benefits for you:

◆ It will show future employers that you can make a big contribution – i.e. that you're a great candidate for the job.

- It will broaden your perspective of working life, equipping you with all sorts of new skills that you'd otherwise never get. And new skills are **always** a good thing because you never know how they might help you.

Find a change project to work on

When you're back at work, try to find out about the change projects that are going on around you. They're quite often called other things, including:

- cost reduction programmes;

- process improvement projects;

- merger integration teams;

- introducing quality drives.

Then, if a change project sounds interesting, find out who the leader of the project is and ask how you can make a contribution to it.

Don't despair if you don't know of any change projects going on that you can get involved with. I can guarantee that someone, somewhere will be trying to make change happen and would welcome an extra pair of hands on the team. The solution may be to network (see Chapter 8) more widely within your organisation to track that change project down.

> *Put your change experience on your CV – it will really make your application stand out from the crowd.*

HELP OTHERS IN UNCERTAIN TIMES

Change at work can have nasty connotations. There can be job losses involved. Or perhaps a new and unfamiliar boss might be parachuted in to run the team that you work in.

Given that most people resist change and see it as a nuisance, the minority of people who both enjoy the challenge of making change happen **and** can help others through it are doubly in demand by employers.

So, what can you do to help your colleagues and raise your profile with the people at the top?

♦ **Listen to people's concerns**. People hate to feel bulldozed by change. Just helping others to articulate their worries will make them feel better.

♦ **Reassure individuals if possible**. Focus on the benefits of change. But each individual will have different anxieties and questions. So try to figure out what each individual will need to hear — because it will be different for each and every person you talk to.

You probably won't be surprised to hear that people going through change are always hungry for information, so:

◆ **Communicate, communicate, communicate**. Try to seek out as much information as possible and share it as quickly as you can.

◆ **Share good news in public**. Success is best announced in groups so that people can congratulate themselves and each other.

◆ **But give bad news in private**. People don't like others to see them when they're feeling weak or depressed. So make sure you tell people bad news in person on a one-to-one basis.

Try to think how you feel when change is being imposed on you. What do you need when things feel uncertain? Then try to translate it into support for your colleagues.

REMEMBER TO

✓ Consider that change is rarely only good or only bad – it's usually a mix of the two.

✓ Get used to change. Only by accepting change in your life will you be able to reach your career goals.

✓ Help your employer and other colleagues through change. Not only will it make you better at dealing with change in your own life, but it'll make you more employable too.

7 Overcome Obstacles

Obstacles are a part of life. Successful people are the ones who don't let them get in the way.

In this chapter:
- **Recover more time for yourself**
- **Learn to say 'no, but...'**
- **Tackle problems**

Numerous barriers can stop you achieving your goals. The most common of these are a lack of time, other people, and physical constraints or impediments.

Learning to overcome these obstacles will help you keep on track to achieving your career goals.

> *If you want something badly enough, could you forgive yourself for not putting the effort in to make it happen?*

RECOVER MORE TIME FOR YOURSELF

Chief among these obstacles is a lack of time; after all, investing in your career certainly takes time as well as effort. So how can you create more time for yourself? There are countless tools that 'expert' time management consultants will try to sell you – organisers, computer programs, indexing systems and the like. But your brain is the best time management system you will ever come across.

Simply apply the following rules to claw back some more personal time:

Ask 'why?' first

If you are faced with a task, ask yourself why you need to do it. Is it something that really needs doing? Will it make a **real difference** to you or your colleagues or your organisation? If the answer is 'no', perhaps the memo or request could just slip into the bin unnoticed!

Distinguish between importance and urgency

At work, we often find ourselves bombarded with 'urgent' requests – messages asking you to call people back straightaway and colleagues wanting to ask you questions. All of these urgent requests can disrupt our thinking processes, meaning it takes twice as long to get something done. But what's the worst that will happen if you don't do it right now? In most cases, the 'worst' will often be inconsequential – which means you can leave it till later to handle at your own speed.

Plan before you begin

Before embarking on a piece of work that you really do think is important and needs doing, take just a few minutes to think about how you're going to do it. What steps will you take? Do you need to consult anyone else or get their help? What materials, information or resources do you need to do the job? Are there lead times on any of the resources that you need – and if so, do you need to try to get those first?

LEARN TO SAY 'NO, BUT...'

The people around us – colleagues, friends and family – can all be a drain on our time. It's easy to get drawn into tasks that we really don't want to be doing.

It is okay to say 'no' when you have a good reason for doing so – even if it's your boss who wants you to do something. Perhaps you've got an important event planned or you're too tired or you don't think it's something you should be doing.

However, saying 'no' isn't terribly helpful to whoever is asking for your time. Think about it from their perspective – they are trying to get something done.

To soften the blow of refusal, think through the following questions:

◆ **Are you willing to make any concessions at all?** For example, you might not be willing to work late today, but you might be willing to come in early on another day. Or you don't want to join the committee on an ongoing basis, but you're willing to give some informal advice to one of the committee members. So, you might say, 'no, but instead I could...'

◆ **Who else might be able to help?** Has anyone else got the right skills, experience or availability to do it? In effect, you're saying 'no, but I know someone else who might be able to help...'

TACKLE PROBLEMS

How many times have you faced a problem that initially seemed insurmountable? Unfortunately, problems will always arise, getting in the way of our goals.

However, adopting a methodical, three-step approach to problem-solving will help you to come up with fresh ideas and improve your chances of picking the best solution:

1. Identify the root cause

Most people tend to skip this step and go straight on to generating options. But that can mean tackling the **symptom** and not the **underlying cause** of the problem.

So use the 'five whys' to look at the real reasons something is a problem. Just ask yourself 'why?' up to five times. For example, a problem might initially present itself as:

◆ 'I don't get on with my boss' – 'why?'

◆ 'Because he thinks that my quality of work is bad' – 'why?'

◆ 'Because he says that my typed documents are poor quality' – 'why?'

◆ 'Because I've never had training on using a computer.'

Bingo – the answer may be to get some computer skills training. So the underlying cause was nothing to do with the boss at all.

2. Generate options

Try to think of **at least** two different ways of approaching the problem. Don't just go for the first solution that occurs to you. Try to come up with three or four different options.

Then for each option jot down a few notes on what the advantages and disadvantages of each option are. If you don't know what the advantages and disadvantages are, who can you ask who might know?

Ideally, if you have the time, leave your list of options for a day or two and come back to it. Do you have any new options to add to your list?

3. Choose a course of action

Finally it's time to choose one of the options.

But if you are at all unsure about which one to pick, why not ask someone else for a second opinion?

> *If at first you don't succeed, try it a different way.*

REMEMBER TO

✓ Give yourself the option of turning other people down. Time is precious and the more of it you spend on helping other people, the less you will have of it to spend on yourself and your career.

✓ Step back from a problem to think it through. Jumping in immediately may only tackle a symptom and not the underlying cause.

✓ Don't forget to think about what you will actually do to improve yourself. Go back to Chapter 3 to revisit your plan of action.

8 Network to Success

It's not what you know, it's who you know and who they know, too.

In this chapter:
- ◆ **Analyse your network**
- ◆ **Prepare to network**
- ◆ **Maintain your network**

People are always the route to success. If you want more opportunities to come your way, the only way to get them is by meeting more people and seeking those opportunities out. For example, many jobs are never advertised – they are filled by word-of-mouth referrals.

If you want to work for yourself, you will need to build up a portfolio of customers and clients. Or you might need to know a range of suppliers to get the right services or products you need at the right price.

Which means that you will need to network. But there really is nothing sinister about it. There are no old school ties involved and you don't have to fawn or be at all insincere to people you don't like.

> *Networking is simply about increasing the number of people you meet, and looking for mutual gain with those people.*

Metcalfe's Law states that the value of a network equals the number of users squared. Applying this law, a network that is twice as large will be four times as valuable.

ANALYSE YOUR NETWORK

You need to think about who you know. Even if you think that you don't know anyone 'important', it doesn't matter because a good networker will be able to forge links with new people, building increasingly useful relationships as you go.

> *In theory, everyone in the world is only six degrees of separation away.*

Start by writing down a list of everybody you know. Think about the many groups that you know:

◆ current and past colleagues;

- customers or clients;
- suppliers and people you've met at conferences.

But don't just stop at your work contacts. Don't forget:

- people on committees, clubs and societies you're a member of;
- college or university acquaintances.

Now prioritise your list according to your career goals:

- What are your **objectives** for networking? Are you looking for a new job? Perhaps you're looking for a change project to get involved in? Or simply advice and information?
- And **who** on your list can best help you achieve your aims?

PREPARE TO NETWORK

You have two choices:

- **Network actively**. Pick up the telephone and ask people to give you maybe just 10 minutes of their precious time to talk or maybe set up a half-hour meeting over a coffee.

◆ **Network passively**. Simply prepare to make a good impression on people that you might meet.

Whichever option you follow, you should think through the five 'I's of networking:

1. Identification

When you meet someone, you need to 'identify' or present yourself. Who are you? What do you do? And, if you are chasing people actively, why are you getting in touch?

But don't put together a lengthy speech explaining it all. Think 'elevator speech' instead. Imagine you are in a lift with the managing director of your dream employer. You only have 20 seconds to talk about yourself before he gets out of the lift. How would you describe who you are and what you do?

> *Rehearse talking about yourself
> in only twenty seconds!*

2. Ice-breaking

It's natural to feel nervous networking – worrying that you'll have nothing in common with the people you meet. But remember that even the most senior person is still human.

And so they will have families and personal relationships. They'll probably hate bad weather and traffic, and more than likely enjoy at least the occasional drink or two! So, try to think about common topics of conversation to break the ice.

3. Impression

We've already talked about making a great impression in Chapter 3. But it's worth reiterating its importance.

You must never let people feel that you are simply using them as a source of information. So show a **genuine interest** in them.

Think about the areas it's appropriate to ask them about:

◆ their job and their company;

◆ their interests outside of work;

- family or acquaintances that you might have in common.

Try to spend more time asking questions and listening than talking about yourself – that's the mark of a good conversationalist.

4. Information-gathering

Whatever your goals, you will have a purpose to your networking. Perhaps you only want to get someone's business card so that you can file their details away for a later date. Or maybe you actually want to gather information about the job market.

So take a few minutes before speaking to someone new to think about the questions you are going to ask them.

- What information are you after?

- And how can you probe **gently** for it without sounding like you're interrogating them?

5. Introductions

More often than not, any given person you meet may not have the information you need. So what you might need is an introduction to someone else – further contacts that you can speak to.

For example, you could say: 'You were talking about X earlier. Do you happen to know anyone else that I could talk to about that?' As long as you are polite, most people will only be too happy to think about other people they might know.

And don't worry about calling on people you've never met. If someone approached you and asked you about your job and your views on your industry, how would you feel? Most people would feel flattered and only too happy to talk.

MAINTAIN YOUR NETWORK

Now that you've invested your time in building up a network, you must put some effort into maintaining it – otherwise people will forget about you.

What can you tell people or help them with? Help them out and they'll owe you a favour in return.

What you do to keep in touch is up to you. For some, a Christmas card may be enough. For others, it may be an occasional phone call or e-mail. 'I was reading an article about the X industry, and it made me think of you. How are you?'

If you change jobs, write personalised notes telling people about your new move. Or ring them if you're passing by and see if they are free for a quick drink.

Consider what is appropriate for each individual that you know – to strike the balance between neglecting people and hassling them too much.

REMEMBER TO

✓ Always be ready to talk about yourself and what you do – you can never predict what opportunities might come your way.

✓ Concentrate on what you think you can do for other people. Make sure you help other people out before expecting them to help you in return.

✓ Keep in touch with your network. Contacts will forget you if you don't continue to show an interest in them.

9 Get Headhunted

*Why look for a job when a job
can come looking for you?*

In this chapter:
- ◆ **Raise your profile**
- ◆ **Understand how recruiters work**
- ◆ **Approach recruitment consultancies**
- ◆ **Hunt on the Internet**

When you eventually feel that you need to find a new employer, there are a bewildering number of companies that will offer to help you make the move. But the ideal job could come looking for you if you have a high enough profile.

RAISE YOUR PROFILE

Headhunters use researchers to track down likely candidates. And they carry out their research by phoning people and asking them about people who might fit a specific role.

Chapter 8 already covered networking, which is one critical way of raising your profile. But there are some other methods you can employ too:

- **Present at seminars and conferences**. Even if it's only an internal seminar, you can get your face spotted by more people.

- **Do well by your customers**. Anyone can be a source of information for a headhunter's researcher. So always take the time to be polite to all the people you deal with.

- **Don't be embarrassed handing out your business cards**. Why should you be embarrassed? What have you got to lose? And it will help a headhunter to track you down more quickly.

- **Send them your CV**. Contrary to popular opinion, you don't have to sit and wait to be spotted. Ring the switchboard of a headhunting company and ask for a named individual you can send your CV to. Most of the time, they will be happy to take a look at your CV, but politely tell you that they 'don't have an opportunity at this time'. But you can be guaranteed that they will keep you on their database for future opportunities.

UNDERSTAND HOW RECRUITERS WORK

There are two broad categories of recruiters:

◆ **True headhunters** are paid on a **retainer**. In other words, they get paid whether they get a candidate into a particular job role or not.

◆ **The vast majority of recruiters** – and some of them will confusingly call themselves headhunters too – will work on a contingency fee or **commission**. In other words, they only get paid if they get a candidate to fill a position.

Put recruiters in their place

So, here are some tips for dealing with a recruiter who might get in touch with a potential job offer:

◆ Ask whether they are paid on retainer or commission (or both) for the particular role they're trying to get you interested in.

◆ Consider carefully the advice of commission-based firms. If they only make their full fee from placing a candidate in a role, they may overemphasise the positive points of a job and neglect to mention some of its downsides.

APPROACH RECRUITMENT CONSULTANCIES

However, recruitment consultancies or agencies can be very useful to you if you know how to manage them.

Some tips for getting the best out of your recruitment agency:

◆ **Ask them about their corporate clients**. Get them to tell you about the kinds of companies for whom they recruit. Are they the sorts of companies that you would like to work for? If not, find another recruitment agency.

◆ **Be honest about what you want**. If you want a very specific role or don't want to work in a particular type of company, tell them. Otherwise a recruitment agency could easily try to put you into any old job – a square peg in a round hole.

◆ **Use interviews with potential employers for practice**. Even if you aren't interested in a particular job, you might want to go along to an interview to polish up your interview skills. (But obviously, don't tell your recruiter this!)

Avoid being seduced by a job

Once a corporate client has met you and decided they like you, a recruiter can be very flattering and persuasive in order to get you to accept a job offer. But remember that they are on commission! So refer back to your life mission (Chapter 1) to check whether the job offer is what you really want or not.

Finally, beware of any recruiting agency that asks you to pay any fee at all – they are more often than not run by people looking to 'get rich quick' by preying on others. These firms are not genuine recruiters and generally have a poor track record for helping people find jobs that are right for them.

HUNT ON THE INTERNET

Websites are increasingly cutting out the traditional recruitment agency. These job resources try to help match your skills, experience and interests with job vacancies. Many of these websites will even e-mail you when a suitable vacancy does crop up.

In addition, these often have further advice and information on the job hunting process. A few have quizzes that help you understand your preferences, strengths and weaknesses better too.

These are just a few of the better ones for you to try:

- ◆ www.workthing.com
- ◆ www.fish4jobs.co.uk
- ◆ www.jobpilot.com
- ◆ www.totaljobs.com

REMEMBER TO

✓ Recognise that there is a huge 'hidden market' for jobs that can only be tapped by networking and having a high profile.

✓ Consider the advice of recruitment companies with care as they often work on commission so may not always have your best interests at heart.

✓ Take a few minutes to go back to Chapter 3 to revisit your plan of action. Reading a book won't accomplish anything unless you resolve to take action!

10 Make a Successful Move

Is that next job what you really, really want?

In this chapter:
- **Interview prospective employers**
- **Negotiate your package**
- **Find your feet in a new job**
- **Have a great future**

It's a great feeling to get a job offer, knowing that you've beaten off other candidates to be an employer's first choice. But don't let the excitement go to your head. Investing just a few days of careful consideration could save you years of grief in the wrong job.

INTERVIEW PROSPECTIVE EMPLOYERS

Before you take that job, should you do any more research to find out more about what it would be like to actually work there?

After all, on the basis of maybe a few interviews, how well can you **really** know your prospective employer?

You should be certain that the job role, the team, and the culture of the organisation are all right for you before you sign on the dotted line.

Some good questions to ask the organisation include:

◆ **'Why do people fail in this organisation?'** This tries to get at the sorts of individuals who don't get on and either leave or get asked to leave. When they describe those individuals, does that sound at all like you?

◆ **'Who are the decision-makers?'** Who will you be working with on a day-to-day basis? And what are their personalities like?

◆ **'What targets will I have?'** Don't be content that you will be given a pay rise with 'satisfactory performance' in six months' time. And what will happen if you don't meet those targets?

◆ **'How important is teamworking here?'** Some organisations expect you to work in teams all of the time. Others may actually expect you to be much more autonomous, providing far less support and expecting you to be more self-sufficient.

What other aspects of a job are you looking for? What does your life mission (Chapter 1) say about the working conditions that you are looking for?

Dig for dirt

When an employer wants you, they often bend over backwards to seem like a good fit for you.

But it's worth finding out whether you really can get on with the people you're going to work with too:

◆ Ask if you can spend a few hours speaking to people in the organisation. Spend maybe half and hour with three or four people one at a time, asking them to talk about both what's good and bad about working there.

◆ Try to organise an informal event to get to know your prospective boss or the team too. People in the bar or over lunch can often reveal aspects of their personalities that they otherwise keep well hidden.

Once you've met them all, try the 'airport test'. How would you feel about being stranded with your prospective colleagues at an airport for 24 hours?

Use your eyes

You can also tell a lot about the culture of an organisation by spending some time wandering around the corridors and open areas of the offices.

◆ How do the people strike you? Are they fun and energetic or merely chaotic? Calm and organised? Or just plain old dull?

◆ What is the office layout? Is it open plan or are there closed offices?

◆ What's the dress code? Do people dress casually or in formal suits all of the time? Do they have Casual Fridays at all?

How well does the office environment suit your preferences?

NEGOTIATE YOUR PACKAGE

We've already touched on the topic of negotiation in Chapter 4. But negotiating around a job involves certain critical elements:

◆ starting salary;

◆ salary review date, targets and expected salary increases for meeting your targets;

◆ your start date – do you want to take a break between jobs?

◆ pension contributions, medical benefits and life insurance;

◆ season ticket loan or company car;

◆ mobile phone and laptop computer.

Other topics you might want to negotiate include:

◆ **Your reporting line**. Who will your boss be? If you like the team but not a potential boss, is there anyone else you could report to?

◆ **Your team**. If you're going to be managing a team, how much freedom will you have to reshuffle or even replace team members?

When you have all the answers, ask for a written offer. Then take at least a couple of days to weigh it all up.

Are you at least 99% certain that you'll enjoy working there and do your long-term career good?

FIND YOUR FEET IN A NEW JOB

The first weeks of a new job can be a perilous time. Your new colleagues will be checking you out and trying to figure out what you're like as a person. And, trust me, they'll be talking about you behind your back.

Your first 90 days will determine the rest of your career within that company.

So how can you avoid starting off on the wrong foot?

♦ **Ask lots of questions**. Don't assume that what used to be acceptable behaviour in your old company will also be acceptable in your new company. So ask to make sure that people mean the same things as you do. And don't worry about people thinking you're stupid at all, because they'll appreciate that you're keen to learn.

♦ **Focus on building relationships rather than completing tasks**. Although it's important to do a good job and do your work correctly, it's vital for you to concentrate on getting on with the people you work with. Ask their advice, listen to their opinions. And try to take every opportunity to socialise with them in order to get on their side.

◆ **Tackle problems sensitively**. When misunderstandings do arise, apologise for them. More often than not, misunderstandings will usually be a failure on your part to understand what is acceptable in the new company.

◆ **Wait before proposing radical ideas**. You don't want to offend anyone by trying to change or improve things too quickly. Wait until you have got good working relationships with the team before making those more revolutionary suggestions.

HAVE A GREAT FUTURE

The exercises, information and advice within this book are only a starting point for your career. Use this book as a guide to achieving a more interesting, satisfying and valued career.

But be patient. Achieving your ideal career will probably take years rather than months. It could involve taking time out to pursue further education. And you might have to change jobs a few times to get the skills and experience you need to reach your goal.

Good luck!

THREE THINGS TO REMEMBER

✓ Don't accept a job offer straightaway. Talk to people within the company. And make sure that the salary package and details of the role are right for you too.

✓ Be careful not to offend anyone when you do join a new company. Ask questions, listen and learn for at least your first few weeks.

✓ Consider your career as a journey, not a destination. So keep revisiting your life mission and goals. Have your goals changed? And what can you do next to help you achieve your new goals?

And finally, if you're serious enough about your career to want to invest some time getting professional advice, why not send me an e-mail at:

ryeung@kpl.co.uk